CALICO DORSEY

MAIL DOG OF THE MINING CAMPS

by Susan Lendroth

Illustrations by Adam Gustavson

TRICYCLE PRESS
BERKELEY

Tricycle Press and the Tricycle Press colophon are registered trademarks of Random House, Inc.

The author wishes to thank the San Bernardino County Regional Parks, Calico's Lane House & Museum, and
Robert F. Hilburn at the Mojave River Valley Museum. Special thanks to Serena Steiner for her kind assistance.

Library of Congress Cataloging-in-Publication Data
Lendroth, Susan.
Calico Dorsey : mail dog of the mining camps / by Susan Lendroth ; illustrations by Adam Gustavson. —1st ed.
p. cm.
1. Dogs—California—Calico—Juvenile literature. 2. Mining camps—California—Calico—Juvenile literature. I. Title.
SF426.5.L46 2010
636.7092'9—dc22

2009032305

ISBN 978-1-58246-318-6 (hardcover)
ISBN 978-1-58246-367-4 (Gibraltar lib. bdg.)

Printed in Malaysia

Design by Katie Jennings

Typeset in Old Claude and Archive

The illustrations in this book were rendered in oils on prepared paper.

1 2 3 4 5 6 — 14 13 12 11 10

First Edition

To cousins Teal and Tristan.
—S.L.

For Adelaide.
—A.G.

Al Stacy almost missed the stray huddled on the porch. Wistful brown eyes looked up at him from the shadows. Al sighed. "Come on," he said, opening the door.

His brother, Everett, was stirring a pot while Everett's daughter, Nellie set the table.

"Where'd you find him?" asked Nellie.

"He sort of found me," said Al, shaking the rain off his hat. Everett dished up four plates of stew over biscuits. Nellie brought one to the wet dog, then sat beside him, stroking his bedraggled fur.

"What's his name, Uncle Al?"

"I think I'll call him Dorsey."

Al's new dog wagged his tail.

Everett ran the post office in Calico, a silver mining town that was teeming with folks riding in on the stagecoach or packing out gear on horses and mules. Dorsey soon made friends with everyone.

He played tag and chased sticks with Nellie and the other school children. Miners fed him bacon and beans, and Dorsey gave their whiskered faces an extra lick clean during Saturday night baths in the barbershop tub. No one was a stranger long to Dorsey.

When silver strikes drew some of the prospectors across the hills to the new Bismarck Mine, Al took Dorsey with him to open a general store. Dorsey missed the comings and goings of Calico. He missed his friends. Most of all, he missed Nellie.

The Bismarck miners missed town, too, especially getting their mail. It was up to Al and Dorsey to fetch a bundle of letters once a week when they hiked to Calico for supplies.

As soon as they reached town, Dorsey would wander off to find Nellie. But once Al began loading the burro to head back to the mine, his dog always reappeared.

One blistering summer morning, Al cancelled their weekly run, declaring, "It's too darned hot, Dorsey. We're staying home today."

Al took a nap at the back of his store, but Dorsey disappeared until late afternoon.

The following morning, Al and Dorsey left for Calico just after sun-up.

"Missed you yesterday," Everett said when they walked into the post office.

"That trail would've been hotter than a giant's skillet," said Al.

"It wasn't for Dorsey," declared Nellie, between licks from the dog.

Everett told Al how Dorsey had come to town the day before, romped with Nellie and the kids, and begged treats from the miners before heading home to Bismarck.

"Next time, wait for me, Dorsey," said Al.

Dorsey didn't listen. From that day on, whenever he felt lonesome for town, he would scamper over the hills to Calico. At the end of Dorsey's visits, Everett and Nellie would shoo the dog home, but, in another day or two, back he'd come, tail wagging.

Everett was sorting through the mail one afternoon when Dorsey walked into the post office and flopped on the floor next to Nellie.

"If Al came to town as often as that dog, we wouldn't have all these letters piling up for the Bismarck miners," grumbled Everett, stuffing another envelope into an already full mail slot.

Nellie looked up from rubbing Dorsey's belly and scanned the wall of sorted mail.

"Hey Pa," she said, "I've got an idea."

The sun was settling on the horizon when Dorsey trotted into Al's store.

"What in tarnation is this?" asked Al, untying a burlap sack from the dog's back.

Al—

If you read this, that dog of yours is better than a burro. He can carry the mail by himself!

Send something back to us.

—Everett

P.S. It was my idea!

—Nellie

For two weeks, Al, Everett, and Nellie sent Dorsey back and forth between Bismarck and Calico, training him to make the Calico post office his first—and last—stop on trips to town. He practiced by carrying newspapers, notes, and even a package of peppermint drops. Dorsey always arrived with the bag tied to his back.

Finally, Dorsey was ready to carry the United States mail.

On the big day, miners clustered in front of Al's small store. One man rubbed Dorsey's ears and promised, "Bring me back a letter and I'll fetch ya' a biscuit." Another laughed, "Bring me one, and I'll give you two!"

Al pointed toward town, "To Calico, Dorsey. Go to Everett and Nellie."

Dorsey bolted down the trail to a chorus of cheers. His feet kicked up puffs of dust that hung in the morning air with the scent of creosote.

In Calico, Dorsey stopped at the post office to visit Everett and Nellie before making his rounds.

When Dorsey returned, Nellie and Everett buckled mailbags on his back. They fit just right.

Nellie said, "I have a surprise for you." She fastened a little leather booty on each of Dorsey's feet. "I made them myself—that trail is rough."

Dorsey gingerly took a few steps in his new booties.

Nellie hugged him hard and whispered, "Show them you're the best mailman—mail dog—they've ever seen. Back to Uncle Al, boy. Home to Al!" Dorsey streaked out the door.

Dorsey's new booties protected his paws from sharp rocks, letting him run the trail even faster.

A chuckwalla skittered away on stubby legs. Dorsey lunged after it, but when he felt the mailbags shift, he turned back to the trail.

Sometimes Dorsey paused to sniff at small dark holes, but he did not stop to dig at the hard-packed dirt.

Halfway down the trail, a prospector called out,
"Hey Dorsey, what you got? Anything for me?"

Dorsey barked a friendly greeting, but did not wait.

He was out of sight before the miner reached the bottom
of the slope.

When a jackrabbit sprang out of the shadows, Dorsey raced after it.

He matched the rabbit leap for leap until the mailbags
slid sideways and bounced against his leg. Dorsey stopped.
Lickity-split, the jackrabbit disappeared.

One mailbag now hung low on Dorsey's side. It tapped his leg with every step. Somewhere he had lost one of the booties Nellie made him.

The air danced with heat. Step, tap, step, tap. Dorsey ignored the lizards startled out of sunbaths. Step, tap, step, tap. Never had he walked the trail so slowly. The mailbag sagged lower.

A shout echoed through the hills: "I see him!"

Mailbags bouncing, Dorsey loped down the rest of the trail, and barreled into Al's arms. Miners whooped and tossed their hats in the air. Someone sloshed down a bowl of water. Al pulled out a fistful of letters.

"Looks like somebody here owes my dog a biscuit!" said Al.

Dorsey barked twice and thumped his tail. "Make that TWO biscuits," Al said with a laugh.

Tomorrow, Dorsey would head back to Calico and Nellie with a new batch of letters. Tonight, the first mail dog of the mining camps deserved as many biscuits as he could eat.

AUTHOR'S NOTE

Photo courtesy of the Mojave River Valley Museum.

DORSEY THE MAIL DOG, CIRCA 1885

In 1885, Calico was a rip-roaring silver mining camp in the rugged hills of California's Mojave Desert. Everett Stacy ran the post office there, and his brother, Alwin, soon opened a small general store about a mile and a half east, where prospectors worked the new Bismarck mines. To carry mail between Calico and Bismarck—sometimes called East Calico—the brothers really did train a Border collie named Dorsey.

For several months, Dorsey carried letters and small packages in little saddlebags. When the mines closed, most people moved away, including the Stacy brothers. Dorsey retired to the San Francisco home of a wealthy mine owner.

There are different stories about how Dorsey began carrying mail. Some said his master became ill and Dorsey took over the mail route for him; others said the dog was trained to travel between people he loved. I believe that Dorsey was a friendly dog, who enjoyed visiting as many people as possible.

As for Nellie, historical records indicate that Everett Stacy might have had a daughter by that name. I included her in the story because I am sure that Dorsey would have made friends with her.

Walter Knott, the founder of Knott's Berry Farm, bought the ghost town of Calico in 1951 and worked to restore it. Once many of the buildings had been rebuilt, he donated Calico to San Bernardino County, which made it a regional park. Visitors to Calico can still enjoy a taste of the old western town where Dorsey once carried the mail.

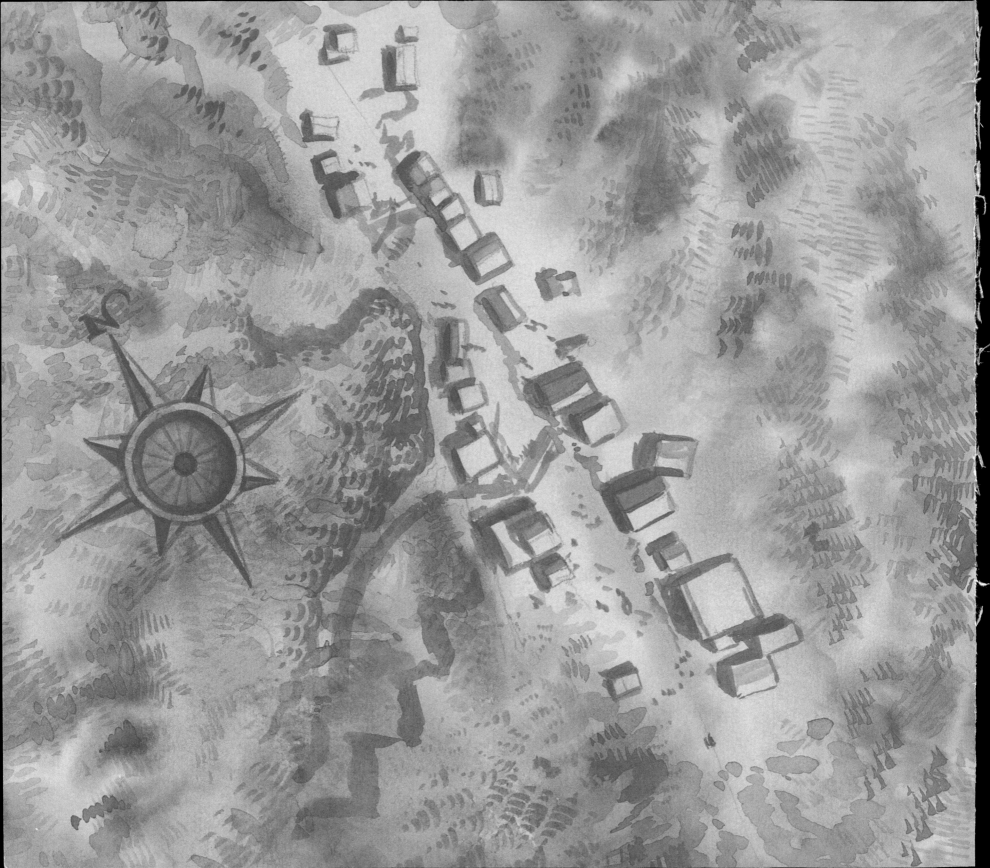